I BELONG TO GOD

A Catechism for Covenant Children

RICH LUSK

I Belong to God: A Catechism for Covenant Children
Copyright © 2014 Athanasius Press
224 Auburn Avenue
Monroe, Louisiana 71201
www.athanasiuspress.org

ISBN: 978-0-9905352-4-9 (softcover)

TABLE OF CONTENTS:

PREFATORY NOTE 5
INTRODUCTION 16
THE TRIUNE GOD 18
CREATION 19
PROVIDENCE 19
CREATION OF MAN 20
MAN'S FALL INTO SIN 21
THE OLD COVENANT 25
THE NEW COVENANT 39
THE GOSPEL 51
ESCHATOLOGY 54
THE CHURCH 55
REVELATION 60
LITURGY 63
SACRAMENTS 65
ASSURANCE 74
CONCLUSION 75

Prefatory Note

This catechism is written by a father who desires nothing more than to see his children walk with the Lord all their days. It is also written out of the conviction that this is exactly what God promises to faithful Christian parents. We must parent out of faith, not fear. We must train our children to understand what God has done for them in making them a part of his covenant and kingdom even in their infancy. We must train our children in such a way that their whole lives will be a grand Amen to their baptisms.

I believe it was Alfred North Whitehead who said the whole history of philosophy was simply a giant footnote to Plato. I'm not sure that's right, but I am sure that the whole Christian life may be seen simply as a footnote to one's baptism. The importance of baptism to one's identity and assurance can never be overestimated.

In baptism, God graciously unites us to his Son and pours his Spirit out upon us. He weds us to Christ and ordains us to his priesthood. As the Westminster Shorter Catechism teaches, baptism is not a mere picture, but an effectual means of salvation.

Understanding infant baptism, therefore, is critical to faithful Christian parenting. This is not to say baptism in isolation guarantees salvation, but God never intended baptism to stand on its own. Rather, as we combine the waters of baptism with the obedience of faith and life in the church, we find that God has already given us and our children every blessing in Christ. This catechism may simply be considered an aid in unpacking the significance of your child's baptism.

Such an approach to parenting, of course, cuts against the grain of our modern Western individualistic sensibilities. I think of Karl Barth's objection to infant baptism: it violently imposes a religious identity on the child without his consent. Sure it does, but this is just what God requires of us in passages like Deuteronomy 6:1-25, Ephesians 6:4, and Proverbs 22:6. Nothing could be more gracious than enculturating our child into the life of God's kingdom.

Besides, a religious identity will inescapably be imposed upon our child. The only question is, Will it be a Christian identity, as the Bible requires? Or some non-Christian identity?

We must reject the ridiculous notion that our children are neutral in relation to God until they reach some mythical age of accountability. We must teach our children what God has done for them in Christ's death and resurrection and what he applies to them through the means of grace in the life of the church.

We are not to try to convert our baptized children; rather, we teach them to persevere in the faith that they have already received in baptism. We are not to treat them as outsiders until they are old enough to make a profession of faith; rather, we enfold them into the life of the body from their earliest days.

It is totally incongruent to baptize a child on the basis of God's covenant promise and then doubt the reality of that promise until the child is older. This practice undercuts everything infant baptism means. It is an insult to our heavenly Father who wants our children to know that he loves them, and it turns the means of grace into means of doubt and confusion. A baptized person is a Christian until and unless he apostatizes. Let us treat our baptized children as the Christians that they are, as elect, as forgiven, as Spirit-indwelt.

Counting and treating our baptized children as Christians is not a matter of pretending or presuming. As John Murray put it, 'Baptized infants are to be received as the children of God and treated accordingly.' For us as parents to do anything less is to simply disbelieve and disobey the covenant. When we tell our children that God is their Father and that Jesus died for their sins, we are telling them something true and helping them internalize their covenant identity.

True, baptized children can renounce their Father and become prodigals; they can reject Jesus as their husband and become adulterers. But having once passed through the waters of baptism, however inconsistent their actions are with that baptismal identity, they are still the actions of baptized persons.

Baptism is an act with eternal consequences for the faithful and the unfaithful. Covenant members who fall from grace can only expect God's harshest judgment. Just as the promises of salvation are for us and for our children, so the warnings of apostasy are for us and for our children as well.

But apostasy is not our expectation. As we trust in God's promises concerning our children and as we nurture our children through teaching, discipline, and prayer, we may be confident that God will preserve them.

Christian parents must continually instruct and remind their children of the status, roles, privileges, and responsibilities that their baptism places upon them. Our children must learn that the Christian story, lifestyle, rituals, and most importantly the Christian Savior, all belong to them.

In baptism they were incorporated into Christ's body, inducted into the royal priesthood of the church, and initiated into the new creation. They must know that these things define who they are and how they are to live. By God's grace, they will grow up never knowing a day when they did not love their heavenly Father. When they do stray into sin, we must 'grab them by their baptisms,' as Philip Henry used to say, and gently bring them to repentance through loving discipline.

I should say a few words about the origin, structure, and use of this catechism. This catechism is basically my homespun revision of the PCUSA's 1998 child's catechism. In fact, several of the introductory questions are drawn almost verbatim from that work, though thereafter fragments from several other more traditional catechisms have been woven in. I took my inspiration from the PCUSA model and revised it extensively, aiming to incorporate seven basic features.

*First, this catechism intends to be intensely **personal**. Some catechisms are just a list of rather abstract definitions. The Westminster Shorter Catechism is a wonderful little document, but it was written by a geometry professor and it reads like it. This catechism, however, is full of warm personal language (a lot of 'I,' 'we,' etc.) that inculcates in the child a covenantal self-understanding. He can't help knowing that the covenant promises are his. Of course, like the Bible, it also includes warnings lest the child grow presumptuous.*

*Second, this catechism is **presuppositional**. It leaves no room for doubt that God delivers on his promises made to the child in the waters of baptism. The child's present standing in the kingdom is never called into question. Its message is clear: God has saved you; now be loyal to him. God has united you* *to Christ; now be who you are. Children need to know that they share in the same relationship with God that their parents have. They participate in the same covenant blessings, face the same danger of apostasy, and stand in need of the same gift of perseverance.*

Parents need to understand this about their children. The covenant promise does not mean we can expect our children to some day have a 'conversion experience.' That turns the Word of God inside out. Nor is the promise simply one of external privilege. The promise made to believing parents is that their children are members of the redeemed community, and that by means of diligent and faithful parental nurture and discipline they will persevere.

*Third, this catechism is **narratival**. The basic form in which God's revelation comes to us is not a philosophical treatise or even a systematic theology, but a story. This is especially how we should teach our children. After a few introductory questions that even very young children can get a handle on, I have tried hard to make the catechism track with the unfolding plot line of the Bible.*

There are numerous interjections that keep the

catechism from flowing as smoothly as it might, but, nonetheless, the narrative of Scripture as a whole clearly emerges. For example, the Ten Commandments are not taken up at the end as a sort of ethical appendage to Christian doctrine. Rather, they are put in their proper place in the story. The post-exilic restoration era is included as a bridge from the old covenant to the new. The Trinity is also taken up in historical, revelational sequence—after the institution of baptism, with its Trinitarian formula. And so on. The point here is not simply that our children will know the story that Scripture tells, but that they will see that this story is their own—that it is constitutive of their identity and their community.

*Fourth, this catechism is **liturgical** in nature. I included questions on the 'divine service' because the way we engage worship (and the way we teach our children to engage worship) is so important. We must see that in worship God renews his covenant with us. We must see that the essence of the liturgy is gift—God's public work on behalf of his people.*

Through the priesthood of Christ, we are drawn into the inter-Trinitarian life of God. The liturgy, properly structured, is nothing less than the gospel in action. God gives freely, we receive in faith, and then we give back, as all is enfolded in a glorious circle of love and fellowship, springing forth from the groundless mercy of God in and through Christ and the Spirit. This catechism enables us to use the weekly service as an opportunity to further impress the gospel into the hearts and minds of our children.

Fifth, this catechism is **intertextual**. *I have sought to pack it with various allusions to and echoes of Scripture and the church's great confessions, creeds, and catechisms. As our children become more educated in Scripture and in the great traditions of their faith, they will find many formulations of doctrine and turns of phrases already buried in their consciousness. I have not included prooftexts, but I hope the Scriptural foundations of the catechism's content will be obvious to all who are familiar with God's Word.*

Sixth, this catechism strives to be thoroughly **Christocentric.** *Christ is presented as the center of the Scriptures and redemptive history. Of course, this cannot be done apart from typology, so this catechism gives our children a taste of shadow/ reality and promise/fulfillment patterns of biblical interpretation. In Christ, all the promises made* *to the old covenant saints are Yes and Amen, the creation is brought to its intended goal, and the kingdom of God is realized. In him, we have election, justification, adoption, sanctification, glorification, and every other Spiritual blessing.*

*This catechism, from beginning to end, keeps the focus on the person and work of the Savior. He is exhibited as the heart of the biblical narrative and the hope of the church through the ages. Finally, this catechism is **catholic**. Sure, there is much in it that is distinctively Reformed, but that is because I believe the Reformed faith to be the purest expression of catholic theology. The Reformers were really Reformed Catholics, and we should be as well. But this means our focus will be on the central tenets of biblical teaching. Thus, I have included the three great pillars of all Christian catechesis: The Ten Commandments, the Lord's Prayer, and the Nicene Creed. Really, if your child knows these three things, he knows everything. And almost as importantly, he is freed from wearing the blinders of a self-righteous sectarianism.*

I have intended to make this catechism rather flexible so it can serve a wide range of uses. In particular, I wanted something that would be of use through the whole course of childhood. The introductory questions can obviously be learned by a fairly young child. Many of the subsequent questions have much longer answers, but parents may find them helpful teaching tools, even if they don't have their children memorize them completely.

I did not write this catechism to multiply catechetical forms. The Reformed church has plenty of useful catechisms, though our understanding of those catechisms is often skewed since revivalism has eclipsed classic Protestantism among modern American evangelicals, giving rise to a pietistic, introspective, individualistic faith. Thus, I truly believe this catechism has a niche to fill in our current situation. The real heart of catechesis is to form in our children a covenantal identity, a sense of belonging to God and to the church. Our children need to be taught who they are in Christ so they can live faithfully in the church, family, and world. May God by his grace enable us and our children to walk with Christ to the end!

—Rich Lusk
Trinity Presbyterian Church
Birmingham, Alabama

INTRODUCTION

QUESTION 1.
Who are you?

I am a child of God.

QUESTION 2.
What does it mean to be a child of God?

It means that I belong to him and he loves me.

QUESTION 3.
What makes you a child of God?

Grace—God's free gift of love that I do not deserve and cannot earn.

QUESTION 4.
How do you know you are a child of God?

Because I am baptized in the name of God the Father, God the Son, and God the Holy Spirit. God made me his child in baptism, just as his Word promises.

QUESTION 5.

Don't you have to be good for God to love you?

No. God loves me in spite of all I do wrong because of what Jesus has done for me.

QUESTION 6.

How do you thank God for this free gift of love?

I promise to love and trust God with all my heart and to live for his glory.

QUESTION 7.

How do you love God?

By trusting, worshipping, and obeying him, and by loving my neighbor as myself.

THE TRIUNE GOD

QUESTION 8.

Who is God?

God is the Triune Creator, Redeemer, Ruler, Lifegiver, Lawgiver, and Judge of all things in heaven and earth.

QUESTION 9.

What is the Trinity?

The Father is God, the Son is God, and the Holy Spirit is God. And yet they are not three gods, but one God in three persons. We worship God in this mystery.

QUESTION 10.

What are some of God's attributes?

God is a spirit, infinite, eternal, and unchangeable in his being, wisdom, power, holiness, justice, goodness, and truth.

CREATION

QUESTION 11.

What did God create?

God created all that is, seen and unseen, by the word of his power, in the space of six days, and all very good.

QUESTION 12.

Why did God create?

For his own glory and joy.

PROVIDENCE

QUESTION 13.

Does God rule over his creation?

Yes, God planned all that comes to pass and governs all things by his wisdom and power. Even the wicked actions of men and Satan are under his rule. This is called his providence. Because God is sovereign, I know nothing can happen to me in body or soul apart from his fatherly care. He works all things together for my good and his glory. He is able to do this because he is almighty God; he desires to do it because he is a faithful Father.

QUESTION 14.

How does this knowledge of providence help you?

This truth should make me thankful in prosperity, patient in adversity, and give me great confidence about the future.

CREATION OF MAN

QUESTION 15.

How did God create man?

God made man, male and female, in his image. God made Adam from the dust of the earth and formed the woman from Adam's side.

QUESTION 16.

What does it mean that we are made in God's image?

It means we are made to reflect God's knowledge, righteousness, and holiness as we rule over his creation.

MAN'S FALL INTO SIN

QUESTION 17.

What did God command Adam and his wife to do?

God blessed them and said to them, "Be fruitful and multiply; fill the earth and subdue it; have dominion over the fish of the sea, over the birds of the air, and over every living thing that moves on the earth" (Gen. 1:28).

QUESTION 18.

What did God require of Adam?

Adam was to trust God and not eat of the tree of the knowledge of good and evil. If he obeyed by faith, he would have been made a glorified king.

QUESTION 19.

Did Adam trust God?

No. Adam stood by and watched as the devil tempted and deceived his wife. After she ate of the forbidden fruit, she gave some to her husband and he ate.

QUESTION 20.

Who is the devil?

The devil is Satan, the tempter and accuser of God's people. Satan was created as one of God's greatest angels, but fell away from God. He is now God's enemy and therefore our enemy. But God promised to crush him under the feet of Jesus and his people, so when we resist him he must flee from us.

QUESTION 21.

How did sin and death enter the world?

When the first man, Adam, turned away from God, sin and death entered the world. In Adam's sin we all sinned, and in his fall we all fell.

QUESTION 22.

What is sin?

Sin is breaking God's law. I sin when I do what God forbids or do not do what God commands.

QUESTION 23.

Are you a sinner?

Yes, I was born a sinner—guilty and depraved—because of Adam's sin. This is called original sin. I sin in thought, word, and deed every day. If I claim to be without sin, I am a liar.

QUESTION 24.

What does sin deserve?

Every sin—even in the smallest, in thought, word, or deed—deserves death and hell forever.

QUESTION 25.

Are you going to go to hell when you die?

No, because Jesus died on the cross for my sins. Sin, death, and condemnation came through the first Adam, but holiness, eternal life, and justification are mine through the last Adam.

QUESTION 26.

How does God deal with us, his people, as sinners?

God hates our sin, but never stops loving us because of what Jesus has done for us.

QUESTION 27.

Must we confess our sin?

Yes. The Bible says, "The sacrifices of God are a broken spirit and a contrite heart. If we confess our sin, God is faithful and just to forgive our sins and cleanse us from all unrighteousness" (Ps. 51:17; 1 John 1:9).

THE OLD COVENANT

QUESTION 28.

What happened after Adam sinned?

Adam's sin brought death and the curse into the world, but God also promised to send a redeemer, the seed of the woman, who would conquer death and undo the curse. Adam and Eve were exiled from God's presence and the Garden of Eden, but God promised to restore them through this redeemer. In Noah's day, God showed his hatred for sin by flooding the world but also showed his grace by saving Noah's family on the ark. Even though man was wicked and rebelled again at the Tower of Babel, God continued to be merciful by calling Abraham.

QUESTION 29.

What is God's plan of salvation?

Before the foundation of the world, God freely and graciously chose a great multitude to include in his covenant and redeem from sin through Jesus Christ. To accomplish his plan, God chose the people of Israel to make a new beginning. They received God's covenant and prepared the way for Jesus to come as our Savior and Redeemer. He would fulfill God's promises to Adam, Noah, Abraham, Moses, David, Ezra, Nehemiah, and all the other old covenant saints.

QUESTION 30.

What is the covenant?

The covenant is an everlasting bond of union, communion, and self-giving love between the Father, Son, and Holy Spirit. God sovereignly and graciously brings believers and their children into this covenant, through Jesus Christ, so that they can live with him forever in ties of love and faithfulness.

QUESTION 31.

What was God's covenant with Abraham?

When God called Abraham, God promised to bless his family, which was later called Israel, and through Israel, to bless all the peoples of the earth. God promised to be Israel's God, and they promised to be his people.

QUESTION 32.

What was the sign of the covenant God made with Abraham?

Circumcision. This bloody sign showed that the promised Messiah, the seed of the woman, could not be produced in man's own strength, but had to be provided by God.

QUESTION 33.

How did God first keep this covenant?

God led Israel out of slavery in Egypt in the exodus and gave them the Ten Commandments through Moses at Mt. Sinai. After forty years of wandering in the wilderness, they were brought into the land that he had promised them through Joshua's conquest. All of this prepared for and foreshadowed what he would do through Jesus.

QUESTION 34.

What are the Ten Commandments?

The Ten Commandments are a summary of the law of God. When God gave them to Moses, he said, I am the Lord your God who brought you out of the land of Egypt, out of the house of bondage:

(1) You shall have no other gods before Me.

(2) You shall not make for yourself a carved image—any likeness of anything that is in heaven above, or that is in the earth beneath, or that is in the water under the earth; you shall not bow down to them nor serve them. For I, the LORD your God, am a jealous God, visiting the iniquity of the fathers upon the children to the third and fourth generations of those who hate Me, but showing mercy to thousands, to those who love Me and keep My commandments.

(3) You shall not take the name of the Lord your God in vain, for the Lord will not hold him guiltless who takes His name in vain.

(4) Observe the Sabbath day, to keep it holy, as the Lord your God commanded you. Six days you shall labor and do all your work, but the seventh day is the Sabbath of the Lord your God. In it you shall do no work: you, nor your son, nor your daughter, nor your male servant, nor your female servant, nor your ox, nor your donkey, nor any of your cattle, nor your stranger who is within your gates, that your male servant and your female servant may rest as well as you. And remember that you were a slave in the land of Egypt, and the Lord your God brought you out from there by a mighty hand and by an outstretched arm; therefore the Lord your God commanded you to keep the Sabbath day.

(5) Honor your father and your mother, as the Lord your God has commanded you, that your days may be long, and that it may be well with you in the land which the Lord your God is giving you.

(6) You shall not murder.

(7) You shall not commit adultery.

(8) You shall not steal.

(9) You shall not bear false witness against your neighbor.

(10) You shall not covet your neighbor's wife; and you shall not desire your neighbor's house, his field, his male servant, his female servant, his ox, his donkey, or anything that is your neighbor's.

QUESTION 35.

What is the main point of these commandments?

You shall love the Lord your God with all your heart, soul, mind, and strength; and you shall love your neighbor as yourself. These are the two greatest commandments that summarize all the others.

QUESTION 36.

What does each commandment mean for us?

The first commandment means we must have no idols, but rather must fear, love, and trust God above all because he is the only God, and he is our God.

The second commandment means we must worship God through the one mediator, Jesus Christ, in beauty, holiness, and reverence.

The third commandment means we must not be hypocrites, but rather speak truly of God and bear the name 'Christian' with integrity and faithfulness.

The fourth commandment means we must give rest to others, and rest from our own labors, as much as possible in order to worship God each Lord's Day.

The fifth commandment means we must fear and obey our parents and all others God puts in authority over us.

The sixth commandment means we must do nothing to harm our neighbor, but rather help and befriend him in every way.

The seventh commandment means we must honor marriage and keep ourselves pure in thought, word, and deed.

> The eighth commandment means we must not take any property that belongs to our neighbor, but rather serve him with all that God has blessed us.

> The ninth commandment means we must not gossip or slander our neighbor, but rather speak the truth in love.

> The tenth commandment means we must be content with what God has given us and rejoice in our neighbor's prosperity.

QUESTION 37.

What is the Torah, or law of Moses?

> The Torah was given to Israel to mark her out as God's chosen covenant people. The Torah did not cancel the promises God made to Abraham, but prepared Israel for the coming of Christian faith, when the covenant blessings would be poured out on all peoples.

QUESTION 38.

Were old covenant saints saved by keeping the Torah, the instruction God gave to Moses?

The Torah served as a tutor, to teach the people they were saved by faith in God's mercy, not their own efforts. Old covenant saints trusted in the coming Messiah, but, if they believed God's promises made in the Torah, they also sought to obey his commands.

QUESTION 39.

How did the old covenant saints keep covenant with God and show their trust in the coming Messiah?

The old covenant saints kept covenant with God by faith and repentance just like we do. They showed their faith by doing what Torah required, especially offering animal sacrifices on God's altar, usually in the tabernacle or temple. These animal sacrifices pointed ahead to the Messiah, who would be the Lamb of God and take away the sin of the world.

QUESTION 40.

Are we under Torah today?

No, because Christ is the end of Torah for everyone who believes. But the Torah is still profitable for us. As we study and meditate on Torah, God makes us wise and equips us to do good works in our church, family, and society.

QUESTION 41.

What kinds of offerings did God give to the people of Israel?

There were five basic kinds of offerings God gave the Israelites: sin offerings and trespass offerings, for the confession of sin and cleansing; ascension offerings, to show consecration to God and entrance into his presence; tribute offerings of grain, to show thanks to God by returning to him a token of what he has given, mixed with human labor; and peace offerings, to enjoy a communion meal with God in his presence. All of these offerings pointed to Jesus, our priest, and his death on the cross as our sacrifice.

QUESTION 42.

How were the animal offerings made?

Only clean, unblemished animals commanded by God could be offered. Animal offerings had five basic steps: First, the worshipper would lay hands on the animal and kill it to show it was his substitute and had to die because the wages of sin is death. Then the priest took the blood and sprinkled or poured it for atonement and cleansing. Then the animal was burned up on the altar, transformed into a gift for God. Finally, there was a communion meal to show God was at peace with the worshipper.

QUESTION 43.

Where were these offerings made?

First in the tabernacle, later in the temple. These buildings had three rooms (the courtyard, holy place, and most holy place) separated by veils. In the rooms were several pieces of furniture (such as altars, laver, lampstand, table of showbread, and the ark of the covenant). All of this was given by God to foreshadow Christ and his church. In these buildings, God made his home among his people. But he also showed by the veils that the new and living way into his presence had not yet been opened.

QUESTION 44.

Do we need to make animal offerings today?

No, because Jesus has offered himself as our sacrifice once and for all on the cross. His blood did what the blood of bulls and goats could not do: He took away our sin and sanctified us. Now, we offer up our bodies as a living sacrifice to God in all of life. These Spiritual sacrifices are acceptable to God through Jesus Christ.

QUESTION 45.

What did God give to the Israelites to help them keep the covenant?

God ordained three kinds of covenant officers. God gave them priests to teach them, make sacrifices for their sins, and lead their worship at the temple. God appointed kings to give themselves in service on behalf of the people, protect the needy, and rule righteously. God sent them prophets to speak his word to them, convict them of sin, and intercede for them. All of this pointed ahead to the Messiah. In the fullness of time, God sent him into the world to be born of a woman, born under Torah, to redeem his chosen people from bondage and bring them to maturity.

QUESTION 46.

Did the people keep their covenant with God?

Though some remained faithful, the people too often worshipped other gods and did not love each other as God commanded. God judged Israel for her sin, and she was driven away from the promised land into exile. Israel's sin showed us how much we all tend to disobey God's law and how much we all need a Savior.

QUESTION 47.

Did God leave Israel in exile?

No. Through the prophets, God promised a restoration, a new exodus, and a rebuilt temple. These things came to pass to further foreshadow what God would do in the new covenant through the Messiah.

THE NEW COVENANT

QUESTION 48.

Who was sent to be the Messiah?

God sent Jesus to be the Messiah. Messiah means "anointed one." The New Testament word for Messiah is Christ. Jesus is called the Christ, because God anointed him with the Holy Spirit to be the Savior who would rescue us from sin and death. As Christ, Jesus is our prophet, priest, and king. In him, all the promises God has made are Yes and Amen and all the types and shadows of the old covenant are fulfilled.

QUESTION 49.

How did God keep the promise to Abraham, and all the old covenant saints, by sending Jesus?

By sending Jesus, God opened up the covenant with Abraham to the whole world. God welcomed all who trust Jesus into the blessings of the covenant. Jesus will reign until all his enemies have been made a footstool for his feet and the earth is as full of the knowledge of the Lord as the waters cover the sea.

QUESTION 50.

Was Jesus just another human being?

No. Although he was truly human, he was also fully God. As the God-man, he lived a life of perfect faithfulness on our behalf, died the death we deserved, and rose from the dead on the third day. This is how he saved us, his people, from sin and death.

QUESTION 51.

Why did Jesus have to be fully God and fully man, two natures in one person?

So he could be the one true mediator between God and man. He represents God to us and us to God. He had to be fully man because God's justice requires that the same human nature that sinned pay for sin. He had to be fully God because salvation is of the Lord alone. Thus, one of the Trinity suffered for us in the flesh in order to accomplish our redemption.

QUESTION 52.

What is the incarnation?

The eternal Word, who was with God in the beginning and who was God, became flesh and tabernacled among us in the man Jesus. In Jesus dwells all the fullness of the Godhead bodily. He is true God and true man: of one substance with the Father and the Spirit in his deity and of one substance with us in his humanity. He is one person, in two natures, without confusion, change, division, or separation.

QUESTION 53.

How was Jesus born?

The eternal Son of God took to himself a human nature in the womb of the virgin Mary by the power of the Holy Spirit. He was made of Mary's own flesh and blood and thus is like us in every way—except for sin.

QUESTION 54.

What was Jesus like?

Jesus was humble (he came not to be served, but to serve), powerful (he did miracles and taught with authority), faithful (he trusted God perfectly on our behalf), and loving (he cared for his people as a shepherd cares for sheep). In all he said and did, and especially in his death on the cross, he revealed God's covenant loyalty to us.

QUESTION 55.

What did he do during his life on earth?

After his baptism at age thirty by John the Baptist in the Jordan River, he began his public ministry. He preached the gospel and called disciples to take up a cross and follow him. He defeated the devil's temptation, fed the hungry, healed the sick, blessed children, befriended outcasts, required people to repent, warned of coming judgment, and forgave people's sins. Most importantly, he established the kingdom of God and the new covenant through his death and resurrection.

QUESTION 56.

What is the kingdom of God?

The kingdom of God is the new creation that Christ established in his life, death, resurrection, and ascension. God now rules his creation through his Son Jesus Christ, the Last Adam. This kingdom is already present and growing, but will not be fully and finally revealed and established until Christ returns at the last day.

QUESTION 57.

What is the new covenant?

The new covenant is the fulfillment and completion of the old covenant. In the new covenant, God forgives our sin, gives us the Holy Spirit who writes the law upon our hearts, and brings salvation to the whole world, just as he promised through the prophets. Jesus proved the new covenant was established when he destroyed the old covenant temple, putting an end to its priesthood and sacrifices, and declared the church to be his new temple and priesthood.

QUESTION 58.

How did Jesus fulfill the Torah and the entire old covenant?

Jesus fulfilled the Torah by keeping it perfectly and bringing the shadows of the old covenant to reality. He broke down the wall of separation, the commandments that divided the covenant people of Israel from the God-fearing Gentiles, so that now all believers are united in one new man and one new family.

QUESTION 59.

How did Jesus teach his followers to pray?

He taught them the words of the Lord's Prayer and promised them that whatever they asked in his name, the Father would do for them.

QUESTION 60.

What is the Lord's Prayer?

> Our Father who art in heaven,
>
> hallowed be thy name,
>
> thy kingdom come,
>
> thy will be done,
>
> on earth as it is in heaven.
>
> Give us this day our daily bread,
>
> and forgive us our debts,
>
> as we forgive our debtors.
>
> And lead us not into temptation,
>
> but deliver us from evil.
>
> For thine is the kingdom, and the power, and the glory forever.
>
> Amen.

QUESTION 61.

How did Jesus Christ prove to be our Savior?

He lived a life of perfect faithfulness for us, and he sacrificed himself for us on the cross. At his death, the veil in the temple was torn from top to bottom, showing the new and living way into God's presence had now been opened. He revealed his victory over death in his resurrection. He now takes away our sin and guilt and gives us his life and righteousness. In him, we have all of God's blessings.

QUESTION 62.

What did the death and resurrection of Jesus do for you?

Because I trust in the crucified and risen Jesus, I am now regenerated (which means I am born from above and share in Jesus' resurrection life), I am justified (which means I am right with God and forgiven by him), I am adopted (which means I am God's child and heir), I am reconciled (which means I am at peace with God and he calls me his friend), I am sanctified (which means I am a priest to God, and he promises to make me grow in holiness and obedience), and I am glorified (which means I have the Holy Spirit living in me and will be conformed to Christ's image).

QUESTION 63.

How are Christ's blessings made ours?

By the grace of the Holy Spirit and the obedience of faith, we are united to Christ. Because we are in Christ, everything he did, he did for us. We share in his election, sufferings, vindication, and exaltation.

QUESTION 64.

How do we know that Jesus is Lord?

After he died on the cross for our sins and was raised to life for our justification, he appeared to his disciples, both women and men. He revealed himself to them as our living Lord and Savior. Through the Bible and sacraments, he continues to reveal himself to us today.

QUESTION 65.

What does it mean that Jesus ascended into heaven?

After his work on earth was done, he returned to heaven to prepare a place for us and to intercede for us as our advocate. He is now seated at the right hand of his Father, and all authority in heaven and on earth belongs to him. His ascension is a great comfort to us because it means one who shares our very nature – our own flesh, made from the dust of the earth – has entered heaven, so that we now have access to the Father's throne of grace. Since the head, Jesus, is in heaven, we can be sure that all the members of his body will be taken there as well.

QUESTION 66.

Will Jesus come again?

Yes, Jesus will come again in power and glory to judge all people according to their deeds and to complete his work of salvation by raising us from the dead, so even our bodies will share in his new life. For now, he remains with us through the gift of the Holy Spirit.

QUESTION 67.

Must you fear the coming day of judgment?

When Jesus comes again, his enemies—those who do not love and trust him—will be condemned to everlasting punishment in hell. But I do not fear judgment day; in fact, I confidently await that day because Jesus has already stood trial in my place and removed the curse from me. The faith-filled good works he has enabled me to do will prove I have a share in his blessed inheritance.

QUESTION 68.

When was the Holy Spirit given to the first Christians?

On the day of Pentecost, the Father and the Son poured out the Holy Spirit—the promised Gift of gifts—and the new creation began to be revealed.

QUESTION 69.

What happened on the day of Pentecost?

When the first Christians met together in Jerusalem, the Holy Spirit came upon them like tongues of fire and a mighty wind. They all began to speak in different languages, to show God would now include all the families of the earth in his covenant with Abraham and the curse of Babel was now reversed. A crowd gathered in astonishment. Peter preached the gospel to them and told them to repent and be baptized.

QUESTION 70.

What were the results of Pentecost?

The Holy Spirit filled the first Christians with joy by revealing what Jesus had done for us. The Spirit enabled them to understand and proclaim the gospel and to live a new life together in prayer, fellowship, and thanksgiving to God.

QUESTION 71.

How do the results of Pentecost continue today?

The same Holy Spirit grants us faith to understand and believe the gospel and gives us the strength and wisdom to live by it. The Spirit unites us into a new community called the church and equips us with Spiritual gifts for the edification of one another in the body of Christ.

THE GOSPEL

QUESTION 72.

What is the gospel?

The gospel is the victorious announcement that the crucified and risen Jesus is now King of kings and Lord of lords. In the gospel, God promises us the forgiveness of our sins, victory over the world, the flesh and the devil, and eternal life, because of what Jesus has done for us.

QUESTION 73.

How should we respond to the gospel?

In faith, which is complete reliance on Christ alone for salvation, and in repentance, which is turning from sin to obey God.

QUESTION 74.

Can you repent and believe on your own?

No, by nature I am dead in sin. The Holy Spirit must give me the gifts of faith and repentance.

QUESTION 75.

Must you walk in good works to be saved?

Yes. Faith without works is dead, but true faith works through love. God has given us his Son and his Spirit that the righteous requirements of the law might be fulfilled in us.

QUESTION 76.

Must you persevere to the end to be saved?

Yes. By God's grace, I will continue trusting in Christ for salvation and repenting from sin till the day I die.

QUESTION 77.

Do you do good works and persevere in your own strength?

No. I work out my salvation with fear and trembling only because God works in me to will and to do his good pleasure. I labor abundantly—yet it is not I, but the grace of God within me. He keeps me strong to the end so that I will be found blameless and faithful at the last day.

QUESTION 78.

What comfort does the gospel give you?

That I belong to my faithful Savior Jesus Christ, who died and rose again for my sake, so that nothing, not even death, will ever separate me from God's love.

ESCHATOLOGY

QUESTION 79.

What will happen when you die?

I will go to be with the Lord in heaven and wait for the resurrection of my body and the complete renewal of the whole creation. These things will happen at the last day, when Jesus comes again in power and glory. This is my blessed hope.

QUESTION 80.

What will happen at the resurrection?

When Jesus Christ appears in power and glory at the last day, our bodies will be raised up and glorified. In the twinkling of an eye, we will be made like Jesus, the man from heaven. He will then judge all who ever lived upon the earth, and all will give him an account of their thoughts, words, and deeds. God's elect righteous ones will be openly acquitted and will enter into the joy of everlasting life, to the praise of God's glorious grace; but the wicked reprobate will be condemned for their sin and will be cast away into everlasting destruction, to the praise of God's glorious justice.

THE CHURCH

QUESTION 81.

What is the church?

We are the church: the people who believe the gospel of Jesus, who are baptized, and who share in the Lord's Supper. Through these means of grace, the Spirit renews us and forms us into his people so that we may serve God in love and live for his glory.

QUESTION 82.

How has God blessed the church?

God has blessed the church by making her a royal priesthood, the body of Christ, and the bride of

Christ. She is his holy temple, the new Jerusalem, and the new Israel. Most importantly, the church is where God himself is found, clothed in mercy and grace.

QUESTION 83.

What does God promise to do for his church?

God promises to be present with his church, to protect her and make her grow. Even when she suffers, God cares for her. God rules over and governs all things for the sake of his church.

QUESTION 84.

Is there salvation outside the church?

There is no ordinary possibility of salvation outside the church. We cannot have God as our Father unless we have the church for our Mother. This is why it is always disastrous to forsake the church.

QUESTION 85.

What are the marks of a true church?

Churches may vary in purity, but even the most mature churches are full of corruptions. A true church is marked by faithful preaching of the Word, right administration of the sacraments, and loving church fellowship (including discipline).

QUESTION 86.

What are the attributes of the church?

The church is one, holy, catholic, and apostolic. Oneness refers to her unity in Christ, which should be visibly manifested in every way. Holiness refers to the church's calling to be God's royal priesthood. Catholicity refers to the universal nature of the church, as she embraces people from every nation. Apostolicity refers to the church's inheritance of doctrine and practice from the apostles of Jesus Christ.

QUESTION 87.

How does the Holy Spirit work in the church today?

The Spirit comforts us with the promises of Christ given in Scripture, even as we suffer tribulation in the world. He gathers us to worship God, builds us up in faith, hope, and love and sends us out into the world to proclaim the gospel, to work for justice and peace, and to obey God in our daily callings.

QUESTION 88.

Why are members of the church called 'Christians'?

We are called Christians because, by faith and baptism, we are members of Christ himself, so that all that is his is now ours. We share in his anointing with the Spirit, we confess his name for salvation, we present ourselves to God in union with him as a living sacrifice, we are seated with him in the heavens, we fight against his enemies (the world, the flesh, and the devil), we enjoy his victory over these enemies even now, and we shall reign with him over the whole creation for all eternity.

QUESTION 89.

What works of mercy does God call Christians to perform for one another and the world?

God calls us to feed the hungry, give drink to the thirsty, clothe the naked, visit the imprisoned, shelter the homeless, visit the sick, and bury the dead. We are to admonish the sinner, instruct the ignorant, counsel the doubting, comfort the sorrowful, forgive wrongs against us, and pray for the salvation of all mankind. By these works of love, we show ourselves to be true disciples of Christ.

QUESTION 90.

How is the church to be governed?

God has appointed officers in his church: pastors (to preach, administer the sacraments, and shepherd), teachers (to explain the Bible), elders (to shepherd), and deacons (to assist pastors and elders, especially in care for the sick and needy). We are to submit to those who have rule over us and imitate their godly examples.

REVELATION

QUESTION 91.

How do we Christians come to know the gospel?

Through reading the Bible and especially hearing it taught and preached in the church. The Holy Spirit inspired those who wrote the Bible and helps us rely on its promises today.

QUESTION 92.

What is the Bible?

The Bible is the very Word of God. It is perfect and true in all it says. It is my highest authority.

Through the Bible the Holy Spirit teaches us how to serve God in all of life.

QUESTION 93.

Does God reveal himself outside the Bible?

All God has made reveals his eternal power, wisdom, and righteousness. But only in the Bible is the way of salvation revealed.

QUESTION 94.

What is the Bible about?

The Bible is the true story of the creation, fall, and redemption. It teaches us what to believe about God and what duty God requires of us. Most importantly, the Bible witnesses to the suffering and glory of Jesus for our salvation.

QUESTION 95.

How are you to respond to the Bible?

I am to obey its commands, tremble at its threats, and believe its promises. The Holy Spirit works through the Word to enable me to do these things.

QUESTION 96.

How was the Bible written?

Just as Jesus is fully God and man, yet without sin, so the Bible is fully divine and human, yet without error. All Scripture was given by the inspiration of the Holy Spirit, as he moved holy men to write his truth. The Spirit has preserved God's Word through the church to this very day.

QUESTION 97.

How is the Bible to be interpreted?

Because the Scriptures cannot be broken, the best rule of biblical interpretation is this: use Scripture to interpret Scripture.

LITURGY

QUESTION 98.

Why are Christians gathered for worship on the first day of each week?

Because it is the day when God raised our Lord Jesus from the dead and gave the world a new beginning. When we gather weekly on that day, the Day of the Lord, God makes our hearts glad as he renews the covenant with us. We celebrate the resurrection of Jesus and enter into his Sabbath rest.

QUESTION 99.

What happens when we gather for worship?

In gathered worship, the Triune God renews his covenant with us. He serves us and gives himself to us through his word and sacrament. Out of sheer grace, God gives us the Son through the Spirit; through the Spirit and in the Son, we give ourselves back to God in praise and adoration.

QUESTION 100.

What is the proper order of worship?

The Triune God serves the congregation in calling, confession, cleansing, consecration, communion, and commissioning.

First, the Lord calls us together, that we might be assembled as his people. He invites us to confess our sin and cleanses us through the pastor's declaration of forgiveness. Then the Lord lifts us up into his heavenly presence to worship with angels and archangels and with all the company of heaven. The Lord consecrates us to his service, by the sword of the Spirit (which is the Word of God), as he proclaims the gospel to us and instructs us through his minister. He graciously feeds us at his communion table. Finally, the Lord commissions us, sending us out into the world with his blessing so that we might be a blessing to others. Throughout the service, we respond in union with Christ our great High Priest and in the power of the Holy Spirit. Our response includes prayer, praise, thanksgiving, and joyous singing. Because God gives what he requires, we are able to believe his word, give tithes and offerings to him for the work of the church, receive the feast of the kingdom, and commit ourselves to serve him and our neighbors in all of life.

SACRAMENTS

QUESTION 101.

What is a sacrament?

A sacrament is a special act of Christian worship in which God graciously gives himself to us through ordinary, created means like water, bread, and wine. We believe that Jesus instituted two sacraments for the new covenant: baptism and the Lord's Supper. Through these sacraments, God offers Christ and his benefits to be received by faith, and marks us out as the church, his redeemed people.

QUESTION 102.

Why did Christ give the church sacraments?

God made us bodily, ritual, and social creatures, so physical, ceremonial, and communal actions are necessary to human life, even in the new creation. The church has sacraments because God marks us out as his redeemed community and knits us together into one body, distinct from the world by these religious practices. Baptism forms the church by gathering us to Christ, and the Lord's Supper maintains the church by manifesting our unity in Christ.

QUESTION 103.

How are the sacraments made effectual means of salvation?

The sacraments are effectual means of salvation, not because of any power in the elements or the one who administers them, but because of the blessing and promise of Christ upon them and the working of the Spirit through them.

QUESTION 104.

What is baptism?

Baptism is the sacrament of union with Christ. Through baptism I am adopted and welcomed into God's family. In the water of baptism I share in the dying and rising of Jesus, who washes away my sins by his blood and gives me new life by his Spirit. I am made one with him and with all who are joined to him in the church.

QUESTION 105.

Why were you baptized as an infant?

Because God chooses to love the children of his people and includes them in his covenant. In baptism, he makes their children his own. Because I am baptized, I must be faithful to God my whole life. My baptism binds me to God and his people forever.

QUESTION 106.

Why were you baptized by sprinkling or pouring?

God always baptized his people with water from above—in the flood, in the Red Sea crossing, and in the ceremonial baptisms of the old covenant. I was baptized in this way because I have been sprinkled with the cleansing blood of Jesus, and his Spirit has been poured out upon me, just as the prophets promised. Having had my body washed with this heavenly water, I am now a priest and may draw near to God in the Most Holy Place with boldness and assurance.

QUESTION 107.

What will happen if you do not live out your baptism, if you are unfaithful to the Lord?

If I fall away, I will be guilty of trampling the Son of God underfoot, despising the blood of the covenant by which I was sanctified, and insulting the Spirit of grace. I can only expect God's fiercest judgment. Thus, I must persevere to the end by grace through faith. I must be loyal to the Lord Jesus Christ who bought me with his own blood.

QUESTION 108.

Why were you baptized in the name of the Father, and of the Son, and of the Holy Spirit?

Because of the command Jesus gave to his disciples. After he was raised from the dead, he appeared to them, saying: "Go and make disciples of all nations, baptizing them in the name of the Father and of the Son and of the Holy Spirit" (Matt. 28:19).

QUESTION 109.

What is the meaning of this name?

We confess there is one God eternally existing in three persons. The Father is God, the Son is God, and the Spirit is God. Yet the Father is not the Son or Spirit; the Son is not the Father or Spirit; and the Spirit is not the Father or Son. The Father was neither made nor created nor begotten; the Son was neither made nor created but was alone begotten of the Father; the Spirit was neither made nor created but is proceeding from the Father through the Son. In the Trinity, no one is before or after, greater or less than the others; but all three persons are in themselves coeternal and coequal.

QUESTION 110.

What is the Lord's Supper?

The Lord's Supper is the sacrament of communion with Christ. In the Lord's Supper I am fed at the table of God's family. Through the bread that I eat and the cup that I drink, Jesus, the God-man, gives me his true body and blood—his very life —and makes me one with him. He forgives my sin, renews my faith, and gives me the gift of eternal life. As I eat and drink the body and blood of Jesus with his people, I rejoice and offer thanks to God for his great work of salvation.

QUESTION 111.

Why do we celebrate the Lord's Supper?

The Lord's Supper is the fulfillment of all the old covenant meals and feasts—the trees in the Garden of Eden, the manna from heaven and water from the rock, the feasts of Passover, Pentecost, Tabernacles, and Purim, and the peace offerings. Jesus came eating and drinking to show his kingdom is one of life, righteousness, and joy in the Holy Spirit. He instituted the Lord's Supper on the night he was betrayed as his memorial that we might call on God to remember what Christ has done for us and give us the kingdom.

QUESTION 112.

How do we celebrate the Lord's Supper?

Just as Jesus commanded: As he was eating with his disciples in the upper room, he took bread, blessed and broke it and gave it to his disciples saying, "Take, eat; this is my body." Then he took the cup and gave thanks and gave it to them saying, "Drink from it all of you. For this is my blood shed for many for the remission of sins." Jesus told us to do this together until he comes again.

QUESTION 113.

What blessing do we receive from the faithful partaking of the Lord's Supper?

We receive the body and blood of our Lord for new life and the forgiveness of sins, and we renew the unity of the church, as the Apostle Paul wrote: "The cup of blessing which we bless, is it not the communion of the blood of Christ? The bread which we break, is it not the communion of the body of Christ? For we, though many, are one bread and one body; for we all partake of that one bread" (1 Cor. 10:16-17).

QUESTION 114.

Is Jesus Christ, the God-man, truly present in this Supper?

Yes, the Holy Spirit makes Jesus present to us in the Supper, so that he is not only our host but also our food and drink. We eat the bread of God from heaven and drink his blood, given for the life of the world, so now he abides in us and we abide in him. This is a great mystery, more to be enjoyed than explained.

QUESTION 115.

How do you partake of the Supper in a worthy manner?

We partake of the Supper in a worthy manner if we come to the table with believing and joyful hearts and if we recognize other Christians as fellow members of the body of Christ with whom we must live in peace and love.

QUESTION 116.

Should the baptized children of believers be admitted to the table?

By all means. The table of the Lord belongs to the body of Christ, to which all covenant children belong, as heirs of the kingdom of heaven. Since such baptized children share in the death and resurrection of our Lord, they ought to receive this holy food and drink for their salvation and assurance, just as children of the old covenant were permitted to partake of its sacramental meals.

ASSURANCE

QUESTION 117.

How does God assure you of your salvation?

Because God is a kind and loving Father, he gives me assurance of his love for me and acceptance of me in many ways. I am assured by the promises of the gospel made to believers; I am assured by the evidences of grace in my life that God sometimes enables me to discern; I am assured by the Holy Spirit, through whom I cry out to God "Abba, Father"; I am assured by my baptism, because through it God forgave my sin and granted me new life; and I am assured by my participation in the Lord's Supper, because through it God proves Christ died for me and has communion with me.

CONCLUSION

QUESTION 118.

How do you summarize your faith?

In the words of the Nicene Creed, written by my fathers in the faith in the fourth century.

QUESTION 119.

What is the Nicene Creed?

I believe in one God, the Father Almighty, maker of heaven and earth, and of all things visible and invisible.

And in one Lord Jesus Christ, the only-begotten Son of God, begotten of his Father before all worlds, God of God, Light of Light, very God of very God, begotten, not made, being of one substance with the Father, by whom all things were made: Who for us men, and for our salvation, came down from heaven, and was incarnate by the Holy Ghost of the Virgin Mary, and was made man; and was crucified also for us under Pontius Pilate. He suffered and was buried; and the third day he rose again according to the Scriptures, and ascended into heaven, and sitteth on the right hand of the Father. And he shall come again with glory to judge the quick and the dead: Whose kingdom shall have no end.

I believe in the Holy Ghost, the Lord and giver of life, who proceedeth from the Father and the Son, who with the Father and the Son together is worshipped and glorified, who spake by the prophets. And I believe one Holy catholic and apostolic Church. I acknowledge one baptism for the remission of sins. And I look for the resurrection of the dead, and the life of the world to come. Amen.

www.ingramcontent.com/pod-product-compliance
Lightning Source LLC
Chambersburg PA
CBHW020624300426
44113CB00007B/766